ATMADEV
JOURNEY TO THE HIGHER SELF

KAVITA SHARMA

Made with ♥ on the Notion Press Platform
www.notionpress.com

Pandit Shri Ram Sharma Acharya - Mata Bhagwati Devi Sharma

"Guru Brahma Guru Vishnu

Guru Devo Maheshwara

Guru Sakshat Parabrahma

Tasmai Shri Gurave Namaha"

Meaning:

The Guru is Brahma, the Guru is Vishnu,

The Guru is Lord Maheshwara (Shiva),

The Guru is the embodiment of the Supreme Brahman,

Salutations to the Guru.

Today, If I am able to write this book and go through these more than two years of journey of self-discovery in order to write this book, it is because of the subtle guidance of Gurudev, **PANDIT SHRI RAM SHARMA ACHARYA and MATA BHAGWATI DEVI SHARMA.**

Thank you for always bringing the light of knowledge in my life and for giving my life a new meaning.

Contents

Contents

Preface

The idea of writing this book came to me two years ago. I was excited to write it, but I had no idea what to write about. I never thought that these two years would become a journey leading to this book: ATMADEV.

The name ATMADEV is not just a name, it is the divinity that reside within each one of us, though we are unaware. It is that divinity within our soul who has the power to make us reach towards our ultimate goal; union of soul (Individual Consciousness) with God (Supreme Consciousness). This journey begins with Self-discovery leading us to Self-Realization and ultimately towards Liberation. This book is the beginning of this journey and who can be a better companion than our own Higher Self. We keep looking for answers outside of us, but the answer lies within us. It's like having a treasure map without knowing how to read it. The treasure is already there, waiting to be discovered, but without understanding the map, you can't find it. Similarly, we have all the valuable resources within us, but we need the right knowledge or guidance to unlock their potential. That guidance and knowledge can be given to us by our own Higher Self.

Listening to our own Divine Self is itself a journey and this entire book is trying to uncover this journey.Everyone's journey can be different from each other, but at the end we reach here. But to reach here we need to keep refining ourself through Sadhna (Self-refinement) and other spiritual practices.

There are different practices and techniques that we can follow to tap into our own Higher Self. But we must remember that reaching towards our Higher Self is a journey, we must be patient and gentle with ourself and enjoy this beautiful journey.

Acknowledgements

APPO DEEPO BHAVA

Meaning:

Be your own light

ᐅᐅᐅ

Thank you ATMADEV, my Higher Self for showing this path of Self Discovery and making me reach closer to my true identity.

ᐯᐯᐯ

I am deeply grateful for the infinite love of divine universal energies for their blessings and unconditional love.

I am thankful to my parents, brother Gulshan and sister Nisha for their love and encouragement. I am grateful to my husband Amit, for supporting and encouraging me in my healing journey.No words can define my gratefulness towards my family,each one has been my pillar of support in this journey,so Thank you.

Shradha my little angel, thank you for bringing healing and spiritual transformation into my life.

Thank you to all my mentors and teachers whom I met in this Spiritual path and who helped me in elevating my journey further.

Thank you to my friends and all my loved ones.

Prologue

This is the journey of an ordinary person who simply wanted to "heal." Not knowing where this journey is going to take her, and how long this journey is going to be, she took her first step on this path...

This path seemed very fascinating at the beginning, she assumed that it will be a cakewalk, and might take few months or maximum a year and then she will be a brand-new person with peace radiating around her, along with love, strength and power she lacked and definitely a boost in her career, perhaps she will become a famous healer or she will be enlightened (though she never knew what it really meant).

With so many expectations and dreams she started her journey of healing. She learned many healing modalities starting from Hypnotherapy, Reiki, Angel Therapy and so on. All these modalities really helped her to move ahead in her life and she started doing her healing meditation such as Grounding, Protection, Chakra balancing, Cord cutting and so on. But this was just the beginning. When she started her healing, she assumed it to be a cake walk with some time-period in her mind, she never thought that this was just the beginning....

According to her, healing was supposed to be completed in a definitive time may be a year or few months, and it will make her a brand-new person, just like we see in a movie. But life is not a movie, and not a nineties movie with a happy ending because there is no ending. In fact, every ending is the beginning, a new chapter, where the challenges also become advanced just like studies when we go from one grade to another.

She thought healing will help her in balancing her emotions and make her super cool about every situation and she will become the best person, whom everyone will admire and appreciate. But she never thought that the journey of healing which she started was never about others or how others will think about her, it is about how she thinks about herself without any filter.

Healing is not about all the good things we need to see in our self but also the grey side. Every coin has two sides, and the story is always incomplete till you see only the so-called good things about yourself. Yes, we must see the positive and acknowledge the positive within ourselves, but a major part of healing involves seeing those hidden and repressed parts which never comes into light. Basically, the good part is always like the tip of an iceberg, but to know yourself completely, you must look inside, which is a major part of that iceberg, of which even she was unaware.

I assume, just like her everyone start their journey of healing thinking that it will be full of beautiful images and feelings, but once we start seeing the thorns in the rose , or the shadow behind a person , we either leave this journey or the only path left is to continue this journey by seeing those hidden parts that is stored in our deep subconscious and unconscious parts of the mind.

Few years back, she thought that if she changes her mindset, it is enough. But what shapes a person is not only the mindset but also the habit. One cannot directly change the mindset without changing the habits or day to day behaviour. In order to sustain the changes, one must bring a change in the habits. These habits or behaviour are like the seeds sown in the soil and we must keep in the mind that these habits that which we are sowing is beneficial and will support us in the journey of healing. This can only be done through **SADHNA**.

ROADMAP OF HEALING

ONE

FEEL THE PAIN

Pain is always something which we want to run away from. Hardly there would be someone who would like to face their pain and suffering. Pain and suffering are things we often try to avoid or suppress, yet they have a way of surfacing when we least expect it, especially when we're in moments of stillness or introspection.

It's like the mind has its own way of reminding us that unresolved pain needs to be acknowledged and processed. While it's natural to want to run away from pain, facing it can lead to growth and healing. Meditation and relaxation techniques can sometimes bring these hidden feelings to the surface, providing an opportunity to understand and address them.

In order to stop this pain from coming to the surface, we numb it. It's like putting a temporary bandage over a wound, but never truly letting it heal. Engaging in constant activity, socializing, or distracting ourselves can keep the pain at bay temporarily. However, it often resurfaces when we least expect it.

Do you know what happens when we supress those painful memories for too long? Just like leakage in a water tank cannot be solved through simply putting some tapes, while tape can be a good temporary solution, it's important to monitor the repair and consider a more permanent fix if the leak reappears. Over time, the tape may lose its effectiveness due to water pressure and environmental factors. This is how pain works, it starts leaking out, in our actions, behaviours, memories, dreams because it wants a permanent fix just like water tank. It wants to be released and it cannot be released until you see that there is pain and it wanted to come out and get released completely. Until you feel the pain, you will keep suffering because it will impact you, your behaviour; you will no longer be the same person that you were.

If you find lot of bitterness, anger, resentment, urge to cry, deep-rooted fears, then there is some pain you are carrying and holding on to that pain will make your life worse as it will change your way of thinking. That experience will make your thinking and belief limited and will make you attract those situations and people who will bring your pain to the surface. Now it depends upon you, whether you want to feel the pain or numb it because it will never leave you, until you feel it. Give yourself the freedom to release that pain which is causing you to suffer and stop this cycle of suffering now.

TWO

FACING YOUR OWN SHADOWS

The path towards healing is no straight path, it is full of ups and downs, sometimes spiral, sometimes like a maze. Each person's path is unique, filled with twists and turns, setbacks and breakthroughs. It's a deeply personal process, and while the destination may be the same—a place of peace and wholeness—the route we take to get there is entirely our own.

What's important is to honour our individual journeys and be compassionate with ourselves along the way. The road might be challenging, but every step forward, no matter how small, is progress.

Many people start out with the hope of finding immediate light and relief. But often, the path to healing involves confronting our inner darkness, facing past pains, and working through difficult emotions. This can be daunting and uncomfortable, but it is a crucial part of the process.

Walking through the darkness can help us uncover insights, build resilience, and ultimately, allow the light to shine even brighter when we reach it. If there was no darkness, we couldn't have understood the importance of a candle in a dark room and that candle alone has the power to lit the entire room and show us the path.

We are only aware of ten percent of ourself, which is the conscious part but the remaining 90 % which is the subconscious and unconscious remains hidden until we decide to heal or go deep in our spiritual journey.

As a child, I was always afraid of Maa Kali and I was not able to understand why her idol was black. But as I grew up and saw negative aspects of my being, when fears enveloped me, I came to the realization that Maa Kali represents change and transformation and how she can transmute darkness into light.

""Maa Kali is one of the most revered goddesses in Hinduism, represents fierce compassion and transformative power. She is often depicted with dark skin, a garland of skulls, a skirt of severed hands, and a fierce expression. Despite her fearsome appearance, she is considered a loving mother who protects her devotees from evil and ignorance. The symbolism in her imagery—like the severed heads and hands—represents the destruction of ego and attachment, guiding her followers towards spiritual liberation"."

May be this was the reason that Swami Ram Krishna Paramhansa was able to see the divinely mother figure (mother of everyone) in Maa Kali and how she helps her devotee with her warmth and unconditional love and provide protection.

Even the shadows are merely the absence of light. They are those discarded part of ourself which we have not accepted or approved and hence kept it hidden in the deep unconscious part of the mind which cannot be reached easily.

These shadows might appear as scary like a ghost or an alien, but this our own discarded parts. We live in a society, where we can only become a good person, but sometimes being a 'good boy/girl' cost our own happiness, we pretend to be someone else. These shadows can also come from our past lives, so nobody can guess how many shadows we might have formed. These shadows can manifest itself in the form of fear, anger, sadness, grief, rage or even more.

Shadows are like mask that we wear in day-to-day life and behind those mask lies the authentic person who we really are, but we don't want to show it to the others as we are afraid that we will not be approved if we show who we are, we are not that perfect person, and hence we keep wearing masks. But this healing journey is not about how others perceive us; It's about our own self.

Are you able to accept your own self?

Are you able to hold the discarded part of yourself again or will you keep it hidden even from yourself?

One thing is for sure, the more you run, the more these shadows will follow you. Now it is up to you to decide whether you want to run away from them or stay right there and look at it.

Sometimes these shadows originate from some deep hurt in your childhood or in adolescent period, trying to protect. You survived that phase of life, thinking you no longer need that role you have taken in order to face that phase (such as showing your angry side). But it never left you, it got stored into your deep psyche.

Now there are only two options left, either again close those doors from where this shadow is coming (probably leading to creation of more shadow) or facing your own shadows.

<u>LOOK AT IT</u>

To face your shadow, look at it closely, observe where it is coming from, observe the emotions beneath it, don't run, listen to it and then let it go. Maybe it will take many days or weeks or months, to face these shadows but once you see it actually, it will slowly start disappearing into the light, because darkness is merely the absence of light and once the light appears, darkness disappears.

It's not an easy process, it will take time, be patient with yourself and don't judge yourself. Try to be compassionate with yourself, you too need that compassion to go through this phase. Journaling can also help in this journey,it will help you to understand yourself more authentically and our emotions can be processed in a better way.

Show some love and acceptance towards yourself. You can pass through this phase. It might seem tough, but you can. Keep working and keep loving yourself and still if you are not able to manage on your own, seek support from a trusted and a loved person. Love and light are always with you!

THREE

SETTING YOUR BOUNDARIES

Imagine a clay pot filled with water. If there is a whole in the pot, water starts spilling out and when there are more than one hole, the pot slowly starts becoming empty or is left with little water compared to the capacity of the pot to hold water. Similarly, our body is also like that pot and the water in that is like energy. Just like the clay pot, our body needs to maintain its energy to function well. Certain people and situations act like holes in the pot, draining our energy and vitality. To keep ourselves healthy and balanced, we need to take care of those "holes" by addressing the root causes and nurturing our well-being.

We must be mindful about whom we are allowing in our life, because certain people knowingly or unknowingly start draining our energy. Not everyone should be allowed in our circle. The more we start healing ourself, the more sensitive we become to others energy. So, we must be mindful of whom we are allowing in our life. Certain people can turn toxic for us and can turn as an obstacle in our spiritual growth. So, we must be mindful of our circle.

Boundaries serve as a reminder for whom we are allowing in our life. Sometimes in order to become a "good person" we allow everyone to access our energy. This can turn as a major obstacle for us.

There are times when we form certain toxic relationships in our life and getting out of it takes a toll on us, but we must come out of this toxic and abusive relationships. But once you come out of it, look within yourself: what was there within you which attracted that person in your life? If you don't heal that part of yourself, the chances are that person might return again or some other person with similar traits can enter your life and this cycle will continue and may become more abusive and toxic, if you don't heal that lack within you.

For example, I encountered certain abusive people in my life who manipulated and criticized leading to self-doubt and low self-esteem. One thing was always common about them they had narcissist traits and they had an art of humiliating you in a way that makes you doubt yourself and sometimes we even start believing that there is something really wrong with ourself. This continued for many years either in the form of my first boss, friend, partner and so forth. But every time it became more worse because just like a video game, the level becomes more advance, and so does the abuse. It can continue until you decide to stop it and bring a full stop to it.

But we must remember that simply ending toxic relationship is not enough. Healing yourself and those limited beliefs that attracted those people in your life is important.

We must know that abuse doesn't necessarily needs to be physical, it can be mental or emotional abuse as well; such as when someone belittle you, make you feel inferior, crushing your self-esteem, creating a negative and stressful environment around you, gossiping about you behind your back and being sweet when you are around, making you doubt yourself, creating drama and scenes every day, projecting themselves as the victim in every situation, instilling fear in you, etc. These are invisible scars which you are given as a gift by them. These things can have long term negative impact on your physical and mental health. You will feel that you have to live with it because your self-esteem goes down. But unless you come out of this abuse, you will never realize that you deserve a better life and relationship.

It's ok to not be ok

You are not sent into this world to only bear abuses, be it physical, mental or emotional abuse. Some people will try to play with your mind, make you doubt your own self, but it's wrong. What made us attract such people? It all sums up to what we deserve. Maybe we thought we deserved it or we deserve such people in our life because we might have seen such people in our childhood or family. But it doesn't mean that we deserve to stay in that mental hell throughout our life. No, we don't deserve it!

You always deserve better and it all starts with you. The moment you realize that you don't deserve this, everything starts changing in both your inner and outer world. So, take the first step to change your inner and outer world. Get out of that toxic relationship. You don't deserve that abuse. Ask yourself: Are you happy? If the answer is NO the take action for a better and deserving life. Change your inner world to bring change in your outer world. We all deserve better and it all starts with us.

Pursuing happiness and a peaceful life is incredibly important, even if it means stepping away from situations or people that don't support your well-being. It's all about finding what works for you and making sure that your life aligns with your values and desires. It's often difficult to take that initial step, especially if others around you don't share the same perspective. But your efforts toward a deserving life will undoubtedly be worthwhile in the long run.

There will be people around you, who might oppose you, but again it all comes back to you. Are you happy? If you are not, then take action. Even if others are saying otherwise, maybe they might have led the same life so they don't know that we can live a peaceful life, away from drama also. It might be difficult in the beginning but at the end all your struggle towards a deserving life will be worth it. All the best!

You are deserving!
You are worthy!

FOUR

FREEDOM TO BE WHO YOU ARE

Every time we are given a choice: either to settle according to societal expectations or to be who we are, our authentic self. Most of the time we fail to live our authenticity and just become a puppet to society's expectation. Even after being the fake person, living life as per society's expectation; we fail to be happy. Why?

Ever thought about an introvert, who recharges and finds peace in solitude rather than in social settings. They can enjoy and appreciate the company of others but find larger groups or excessive social interaction draining. This preference for quiet and limited interaction doesn't equate to disliking people or being anti-social. Rather, it's about how they best function and thrive. Is there any problem in living like that?

Living a quiet life with fewer people around allows them to engage more deeply in their thoughts, hobbies, and interests. It gives them the space to reflect and the freedom to be themselves without the constant need for social performance. Introverts often have a rich inner world and can be highly creative and thoughtful. It's important to respect and understand these differences in personalities. A quiet, introspective life can be immensely fulfilling for those who prefer it.

But the question is, why does everyone have to judge or push him to be an extrovert? Just like extrovert are accepted in society, why can't we accept an introvert just the way he is. Being an introvert is not a psychological disorder or some ailment. There is nothing wrong in being an introvert, just like there is nothing wrong in being an extrovert.

An introvert loves to spend time with himself, but because of constant judgement by others he forces himself to change, only to create a war within himself.

In the path of spirituality, it is often emphasized to go inward that **Spirituality is an inward journey** and the person needs to spend time with himself, to observe, to introspect and to meditate. This can only be possible when the person is willing to spend some alone time with self. The more we are surrounded with people and trying to change ourself in order to fit in to other's expectations, the more far we go from ourself and more difficult it becomes to meditate, which is the most important part of the Spiritual world. Everything is incomplete without going inward.

So next time when you are asked to choose between your authentic self and the societal role, choose your own freedom; the freedom to be who you are; freedom to be your authentic self and that is how you remain true to yourself and feel deep satisfaction when you choose yourself; the authentic self without any masks.

FIVE

WEAR YOUR ARMOUR

There will be situations in your life when we feel nobody around us, where we will be all alone with no support. Some might make you doubt yourself according to their belief system. You will doubt your oneself and you will not get any assurance of whether what you are doing is right or wrong. But the moment you give up and doubt yourself, you will never be able to listen to your inner voice, which might tell you something different than what you have heard till now. Yes, that inner voice exists. Every time we don't listen, it stops whispering and there comes a time when it stops whispering completely, because it gets defeated by oneself, our own inner critic.

If you want to listen to that inner voice, you need to pay heed to what it says and follow it, take action. If you don't, it will disappear. But once you start trusting it, despite everyone opposing you and your thoughts and action, you will give rise to a **warrior** inside you.

We are not here to always be victim to a situation, but we are here to change our situation and to become a warrior, wearing the armour of change and transformation. Somebody has to become strong and give rise to that warrior we were always meant to be. Stop being victim to a situation and transform your situation and struggles like a warrior, never give up on yourself. We are stronger than we think. We have simply forgotten that.

"Goddess Parvati, one of the principal deities in Hindu mythology, is known for her various forms, including the fierce Goddess Durga and Kali. According to the mythology, Parvati's transformation into Durga signifies the ultimate power and divine energy that manifests to combat evil and restore righteousness. This transformation represents the Shakti (divine feminine power) that is capable of destroying the darkest forces and it's a symbol of empowerment, courage, and the triumph of good over evil."

We are all powerful souls, and we are here to remind ourself of our own power, just like gold retains its inherent value and shine no matter how much dust covers it, we too possess an innate power and light that remains untouched by external circumstances.

It's a reminder of the strength and potential within us, waiting to be rediscovered and harnessed. Whether through moments of introspection, spiritual practices, or acts of kindness and courage, we can reconnect with that inner power and let it shine through.

So, **"Awaken your inner warrior. Wear your armour and claim your strength and power back."**

SIX

SHEDDING THE OLD SKIN

A snake shed its skin two-four times every year and during this process, snake feels uncomfortable, but once it shed its skin, it becomes comfortable again. Similar to the snake, we must also shed our old skin and what is this old skin?

These are our limiting beliefs, conditionings that we have learned since we were child, but not everything is truth and sometimes those things that we have learned in our past creates a hinderance to our future growth because we don't want to change our beliefs and thoughts as it makes us uncomfortable. But sometimes those thoughts and beliefs keeps us caged like a fish in a small river who is afraid to unite with the sea. But this spiritual journey is about becoming one with the sea, coming out of the comfort zone and realizing we were never different from the sea (God), we were always the same, but it was our limiting belief about oneself such as I am small or inferior or impure or underserving or unworthy or powerless or unloved or unheard or undeserving, etc. that keeps us separate from the Divine, unconditional love of the infinite universe.

This entire journey is about becoming comfortable in being uncomfortable, we have to challenge our thoughts and beliefs often, we have to move beyond our conditioning, we have to allow ourself to merge into that infinite sea of unconditional love, where we will be able to find our true self, the one we are unaware of, the one which will end all the suffering because the root of suffering is the belief that we are separate from the universe. But the reality is

"SOHAM
I AM THAT I AM
The universe exists within me, as much as I exist in the Universe."

PATHWAY TO THE HIGHER SELF

SEVEN

SADHNA

Sadhna is a spiritual gift which one must practice bringing a permanent change in our psyche.

Refinement of personality through various tools is known as Sadhna.

These tools didn't need to be something very hard; it can be easy to adopt changes which helps us to sustain the changes that we are making in our *samskaras;* impressions in our mind. Samskaras are those impressions which has been stored since our birth, it might be coming from our parents or the one which we have learned in childhood, or it can also come from previous births. So, you can now understand that these *samskaras* are deeply rooted in our unconscious mind, some of which are useful and some harmful. Those *samskaras* which are helpful can lead to our growth. Whereas those samskaras which are harmful or useless can work as a hinderance towards our spiritual and healing path.

This is where Sadhna plays an important role, removing the harmful *samskaras* and sowing the seeds of positive and uplifting *samskaras.*

Sowing the seeds through Sadhna

Sadhna must be an important part of a person's life, if they need to make their spiritual development. It is not necessary that we must do severe penances or take challenging task. For each person their Sadhna can be different. For some people their Sadhna can be washing utensil or cleaning their own space and for some it can be simple act of having early bath in the morning and doing meditation. It is up to us to decide what is going to be our sadhana, may be combination of 2-3 tasks together or may be one simple act of washing your own plate after eating.

It can also be included in your morning routine as it's our morning routine which sets our day. So whether you want to start your day with bed tea and mobile scrolling or you want to begin your day with gratitude and doing positive activities such doing yoga, meditation or chanting, it depends upon you.

But our Sadhna varies depending on what suits us and what is more beneficial for us. If we are not sure, what should we do as our sadhna, then seek guidance from the universe, if you want to bring change in your life on a positive note, universe will always support and guide us.

> "I have seen Mataji, Mata Bhagwati Devi Sharma doing her each work as Sadhna, whether it was washing utensil, cooking food or serving food to thousands of devotees with unconditional love."

When we are present in that moment and perform that work without any ego or considering each work as equally important despite it looking big or small, that is Sadhna. It is something we do for ourselves not for others, because this not only helps us in refining our personality but also helps us in sustaining the positive qualities within us. Doing our own work is also Sadhna. This doesn't have to be vast; it can be simple day to day activities. We must remember that without Sadhna, it becomes difficult to sustain our spiritual journey. Sadhna keeps us in check and helps us to remain humble. It serves as a torch in a dark tunnel helping us to cross the tunnel without being afraid.

EIGHT

DECLUTTERING

You must have heard the word decluttering often. This is an important aspect of healing. Decluttering which can simply be described as clearing the space, should be an important aspect of life.

Imagine yourself carrying bags full of clothes on your back for many hours, it will hurt, right? Similarly, we keep on holding to so many things in our life in the form of old, useless bags. These bags keep on staying in our home in a storeroom and it keeps on increasing every year, until we start checking which of the things in the bag are useless and needs to be discarded. Often, we do that once in a year during Diwali where we clear certain piles of garbage stored in our home. Similarly, we hold to many piles of heavy emotions of our past in the form of hurt, sadness, fears, pain, grief, depression, anger, shame, etc. Do we ever think to clear this garbage from our mind?

We must clear these old hurt and emotions to clean our mind. During Diwali festival, when we clean our home, it feels light and then we decorate it and make our home look beautiful. Similarly, when we clean our mind by the art of letting go, we ae able to decorate our mind with new experiences which are useful and gives us happiness. Therefore, next time when we clean during Diwali, we should also clean our mind because if the mind is not clean, we cannot bring new opportunities and beautiful experiences in our life. In fact, Diwali come once in a year, but we should make it a habit to clean our home and our mind at least once in a month.

Some healers, declutter their home every full moon, where they not only clean their space and remove unnecessary items but also clean their mind as moon represents our feelings and emotions, which becomes full during Full moon and some people feel over whelming emotions during that time. Therefore, decluttering serves as an important part of healing.

NINE

FASTING

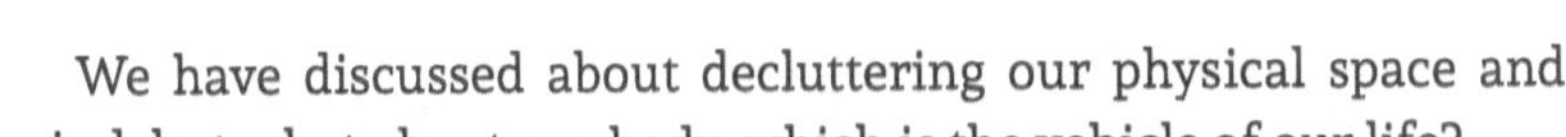

We have discussed about decluttering our physical space and mind, but what about our body, which is the vehicle of our life?

Are we thinking about our body and its health?

If the body is not healthy, then it effects our mind and vice versa. A very important aspect of keeping our body healthy is through FASTING, either once in a week or may be every fifteen days.

Our digestive organs keep on working without any rest. Fasting can help in detoxification of the body, give rest to the digestive organs and can also help in maintaining good health. Research has shown that intermittent fasting can lead to improvements in health conditions such as obesity, diabetes, cardiovascular disease, cancers and neurological disorders, according to Mark P. Mattson, Ph.D., formerly of NIA's IRP and currently a neuroscientist at the Johns Hopkins University School of Medicine.

Therefore, we must take care of our body through fasting or if one is unable to do full day fasting, they can do intermittent fasting of 12-14 hours. When we allow our body to rest with the help of fasting, we help in improving our health. In Yogic tradition, there is a detoxification process which cleanse the intestinal tract partially known as Laghu Shankha Prakshalana (LSP), which improve our digestion and removes stored toxins from our body. But this is not recommended for everybody.

If someone cannot do fasting, they can have fruits, or instead of having two meals can have one meal in a day (once in a week).

One important aspect of remaining healthy is eating according to our biological clock i.e., by finishing our dinner early by sunset, because just like the sun, our body has digestive fire which slows down after sunset hence making the digestion process slow. Therefore, eating according to the sun's intensity such as eating heavy meal in the afternoon and light meal in the evening or night can aid in improving our physical health i.e., following the circadian rhythm diet.

TEN

SANKALPA SHAKTI

During the time of New Year, we often take resolution for the New Year such as we will lose weight, go to gym, eat healthy diet, etc. But after few days or let's say after a month, we don't even remember that we have taken a resolution.

Sankalpa is a Sanskrit word that means a vow, intention, or determination. It is a powerful tool in yogic and spiritual practices, often used to set a positive intention or resolve at the beginning of a ritual, meditation, or practice. A Sankalpa is typically a short, positive affirmation that you repeat to yourself, aligning your mind and heart towards your deepest aspirations.

Creating a Sankalpa involves:

1. 1. Reflecting on what you truly desire or need in your life.
2. 2. Crafting a simple, affirmative statement in the present tense.
3. 3. Repeating it with conviction, especially during moments of stillness or meditation.

In India (Vedic tradition) we take Sankalpa with *Akshat* (rice) and *pushpa* (flower) in our hand and recite mantras and take a Sankalpa during that time under the divine grace of that particular deity or God. We often call it as *Sankalpa Shakti* because when we take a firm determination under the divine guidance, even universe helps us in fulfilling that, Sankalpa.

Let's say when we perform any Anusthan (for example nine days Navratri Anusthan or Gayatri Anusthan), we follow it without any discomfort and everything happens smoothly such as doing fasts and reciting fixed number of mantras (such as 27 rosary of Gayatri mantra per day) because during that time period, we have taken a Sankalpa, with a firm determination and the universe itself supports us. To understand it easily, it's our own power of mind which we underestimate at times. Our own mind sets a goal with firm determination and we stick to it 90-99 % of the time. Our own will power supports us along with divine support by the universe.

But even for Sankalpa to fulfil, we must commit ourself to that set goal. It's not always necessary to sit and recite mantras to take Sankalpa. Basically, Mantras have strong vibrations which helps us to fulfil our Sankalpa. But if we have strong will power, we can take Sankalpa mentally as well. It all depends on us. Our will power, our mental strength.

SANKALPA AND SHAKTI

- When we take Sankalpa, it gives us Shakti (power)to complete that set goal.
- Sankalpa itself is so strong that it becomes Shakti (power).

Both ways it is the power of Sankalpa Shakti which can help us to reach a desired goal. But we should first start with a small goal in mind and then proceed towards a larger goal, going one step at a time.

Sankalpa Shakti, or the power of resolve, is a profound concept in Indian philosophy and spirituality. It signifies the ability to channel one's willpower and intent toward achieving goals and manifesting desires. It's often associated with the practice of setting positive intentions and committing oneself to personal and spiritual growth.

Drawing upon Sankalpa Shakti can help you harness inner strength and focus your energy on overcoming challenges and achieving success. Whether you are looking to make a positive change in your life or deepen your spiritual practice, cultivating this power of resolve can be a transformative journey.

Sankalpa Shakti can not only bring material benefits, but also spiritual and personal growth. Now it is upon us that what is our purpose. It can be weight loss, becoming a Yoga Therapist, writing a book, gain inner peace or connect with your higher self. It also helps us in reaching that goal by also showing us the path we need to achieve that goal as if the entire universe conspires on our behalf to attain that goal. But we must remain aware of our Sankalpa always. By consistently integrating your Sankalpa into your daily life, you keep your intention alive and active, guiding you towards your goal.

ELEVEN

THE REAL SATSANG

A person who is new in the path of Spirituality is like a wet soil and thus he needs to be cautious of his company because the company in which a person lives, shapes a person, just like how the wet soil is going to form a pot. Just as wet soil takes the shape of the mould it's placed in, a person on the spiritual path can be profoundly influenced by their surroundings and the people they engage with. It's so important to choose one's company wisely and surround oneself with positive, uplifting influences.

Our Rishis and Sages have emphasized on Satsang often. Satsang refers to the company that we keep and with whom we spend most of our time. A child imitates whoever he sees and tries to become like that. Similarly, if an adolescent, though good-natured starts staying in the company of a bad group, who takes cigarettes and has drinking habits will have ninety percent of chances of becoming like his group members. This is applicable to all of us. Thus, we must be alert about the people with whom we spend our time. Satsang is referred as the company of good people or spiritual people. When we stay in their company, we not only start imbibing their good quality but also their presence has a positive influence on our personality. One more benefit includes that any doubt arising in this path can also be resolved with their experience and guidance.

Therefore, Satsang plays a vital role in shaping our personality and help us to alleviate our spiritual journey.

Similarly, if we are surrounded with people who are not in alignment with our purpose, they will indirectly distract us from our goals and without even realizing we will get trapped in worldly affairs which not only lower our vibration but also will take us away from the goals. This will lead to further dissatisfaction with life.

The saying that "a man is known is known by the company he keeps" perfectly applies on this context. We must remain alert with what kind of people we are surrounding ourself, keep asking yourself, dose this person alleviate my journey? or Am I getting distracted?

TWELVE

SWADHYAYA

Gurudev Pandit Shri Ram Sharma Acharya has always placed utmost importance on Swadhyaya and Satsang.

One of the pledges given by him in Yug Nirman Movement (Construction of Era) which motivate us to concentrate on self-reformation is:

> "'With a view to keeping our minds free from the inrush of negative thoughts and emotions, we will adopt a regular program of study of ennobling and inspiring literature (swadhyaya) and of keeping the company of saints (satsang)'."

Mind can be considered like a monkey who keeps jumping from one thought to another just like a monkey who keeps jumping from one tree to the other. We must take measures to bring stability to our mind. In no time, mind can create hundreds of imaginary situations and lead us to deep suffering and pain, without even us realizing that it was the creation of our mind.

To control this monkey mind, one has to take the initiative as mind can become our greatest friend or biggest enemy. It depends upon us. If we keep our mind engage, then we can turn it into our friend and lead it to positive direction, otherwise it can become our greatest enemy making us suffer throughout our life.

To control our mind, we must include Swadhyaya and Satsang. Swadhyaya refers to reading good, spiritual and uplifting books which can nourish our mind and sow seeds of positivity. When we read such positive and uplifting books it guide us in our spiritual journey and even the doubts and obstacles that we face can be overcome. We must keep in mind to bring Swadhyaya in our daily practice.

To begin Swadhyaya journey, one must keep in mind to read those books which are inspirational or self-help or about Sanits or spiritual people. One must avoid reading those books which are not useful for our mind specially involving violence and hatred.

Swadhyaya

Thus, we should choose the books wisely. A book can illuminate our soul and help us tom remain consistent in the spiritual path. Even in scriptures utmost importance has been given to Swadhyaya and Satsang. These two are incredible powerful practices that can build a strong foundation for our Spiritual growth.

THIRTEEN

SIT WITH YOURSELF

We humans have a tendency to always stay busy with something or the other. We cannot sit idle even for a second, and with the advancement of technology, we have become technologically handicapped. We cannot live without our phones or other gadgets. In fact, even when we go for a morning walk, we feel the need to carry our phones, either to talk with someone or to listen to some good music. While it's not bad to enjoy music or have conversations, it's also important to take a moment to appreciate nature during our walks. Notice the beautiful trees, colourful butterflies, feel the fresh morning air, or simply focus on one thing at a time, enjoying the essence of the morning walk.

Essentially, we have developed an aversion to spending time with ourselves without any gadgets, simply sitting and doing nothing. For most of us, this seems impossible. However, the true beauty lies in spending time with ourselves, sitting quietly without any distractions. But what should we do when we sit with ourselves?

- **Chintan-Manan** also known as **self-reflection**. Trying to absorb all those essential information that we have gained from *Swadhaya* and *Satsang*, reflect on it. Observe yourself and try to be a mirror for your own self and see where you are; see your strengths and weaknesses. Just be an observer and see where you are, without judging yourself; without forming any opinion about yourself. When we sit with ourself, information starts coming on its own, wisdom starts reaching our inner self; nourishing our soul and allowing our soul to shine like it was always meant to be. With the help of Chintan-Manan, all the dusts and garbage surrounding our soul starts to fade away and the spark of our soul starts shining, paving the way towards AtmaDev.

- **Journaling** can also help us in Chintan-Manan. Sometimes when we are not to able to think clearly, writing can help us to clear our mind, bringing some wonderful realization and insight which was kept hidden in the daily chores of life.

- **Mediation** is a beautiful technique of sitting with your own self and the most difficult thing to do as well. When we meditate, we again nourish our soul and creates a beautiful pathway for our higher self to connect with the universal energies: *Parmatama*. But most of us face a difficulty in meditating, that we are unable to concentrate. But this is common concern for most of us. Our monkey mind starts bringing all the past memories and future worries whenever we sit for meditation, making it more difficult and finally we leave it after repeated attempts to mediate. But have you seen a child learning to walk, he keeps falling and tries more harder again, until he learns to walk. Similar technique applies with meditation. Here we need to train our mind with repeated attempt to meditate and this will happen in few days or months, it might even take a year or more than that. But consistency is the key in meditation. One must keep practicing meditation regularly, at the same time and at the same place with less distractions. We can seek the help of a guided meditation in the beginning or chanting meditation. Starting meditation journey with OM Chanting can be helpful for the beginners. The most beautiful realization about meditation is that even if we think nothing is happening, but still, something is happening, trust the divine; you are sowing the seeds of divinity within you, don't stop in between. Keep repeating it every day and the seeds of your divinity will grow into a beautiful tree, radiating your entire aura with that divinity. So do not stop in between.

Though there may be many resistances in between, still sit with yourself. Chintan Manan should be a part of our daily life.

FOURTEEN

OBSTACLES IN SPIRITUALITY

In the path of Spirituality, we face certain hurdles because of which we sometimes remain stuck in the same phase for a long time until we break free from it with the help of consistency in our practice. But this consistency gets challenged when we face obstacles in our practice and either we leave it or become doubtful about our practice, which keeps us stagnant with no further progress in the spiritual path. In order to recognise these obstacles, we must first know about it and through awareness we can get out of these challenges.

The most common obstacle that we go through in the path of Spirituality is *lack of belief* either on the teacher (Guru), or on the practice itself. When we show disbelief and doubts the practice or the teacher, it makes us loose our interest in the practice and we get stuck in a maze. One must first trust the teacher and their authenticity before beginning the practice and once they become sure, then they should begin with the practice.

Our own disposition (or nature) can also form an obstacle in our spiritual path. Consider a person who has always been lazy and procrastinating throughout their life. If you expect to become a conscious person and wake at 3 or 4 AM in the morning and do all the spiritual practices assuming a magic will happen, then this expectation is also a hurdle because expecting a person who has always been lazy and who loves to sleep in morning, to change in just one or two days of practice is a foolishness. Even setting such difficult target can lead to failure in the very beginning. A goal in any sphere should be set considering the disposition of the person and should be set in small steps instead of taking a big step towards your goal. Therefore, one must carefully set the desired practice and should break it in step-by-step process making it easier and which will not lead to failure.

Some challenges or the other always come in our life. But we should be aware about our goal and always remain conscious of our aim. Sometimes we lose our aim, in fact forget about it with certain challenges of life such as sudden health issues, or sickness in family, some financial trouble, relationship issues, and with some other priorities of our life. These situations are unavoidable and takes so much of our time and energy that we forget our spiritual goals or ultimate aim of our life and without even realizing we again go far from that goal and remember these during our death bed when we cannot do anything.

Challenges and hurdles will come, but sometimes it will leave us either ahead or deviate us from our real destination. The choice lies with us, whether we want to move ahead or get perplexed in the suffering of life. Do we want to become an alchemist by transforming our life or just move ahead like the wave of the sea without any direction. The choice always lies in our hand.

FIFTEEN

REFRAIN FROM JUDGEMENT

A very dangerous obstacle in the path of Spirituality is Judgement and we must try to keep this behaviour in check. Judgement is something we all have done and since when nobody knows, because from the moment we are born we hear so many people passing judgement based on our appearance, behaviour, habits and so on. And as we grow up it becomes a part of our behaviour too because children learn from observation and when this behaviour becomes a apart of our behaviour nobody knows as it is ingrained in our behaviour and it becomes an automatic response in different circumstances and nobody ever think that this habit is very harmful and an obstacle to our own spiritual growth.

We all are a part of the universe(uni-verse) which means we are our own mini-verse (part of the infinite universe), so whatever is there in the universe is also a part of us, though we are unaware of it as it is stored in the unconscious aspect of the mind. So, the moment you judge someone else, you are actually inviting that quality (either good or bad) within you. For example, the moment you judge a mother that how can she behave so badly with her child, how can she be so cruel and rude and bingo. You have unintentionally invited the same quality within you by asking the universe, how can that person do this. So judgement is a major obstacle because though you want to go high into your spiritual journey, the more you are pulled back due to this habit of judgement. Imagine that you want to pluck rose flowers which are very beautiful to look at and has a mesmerizing fragrance, but while picking those rose flowers, we must be careful about the thorns in it. Despite its beauty it still contains thorns. Similarly, we all also have the dualities good and the bad within us. The moment you judge you are inviting those bad or dark aspects to rise up within you which are hidden in your deep unconscious mind. The more you judge, the more you become like that. The more you accept and find blessings in life, the more blessings you see in your life.

There is also a different perspective to the habit of our judgement. In Bhagvad Geeta, Lord Krishna has shown his Virat Rup to Arjuna. Do you know what was that?

The concept of Lord Krishna's "Virat Rup" in the Bhagavad Gita is both profound and awe-inspiring. The "Virat Rup" is often referred to as Krishna's "universal form" or "cosmic form." It represents the infinite and omnipresent nature of the Divine, showcasing the interconnectedness of all creation and existence. It was the entire creation, the universe itself. So, the moment we are judging someone and passing comments on others, we are judging our creator, God itself. Now do you really want to do that?

Nobody tells us that this habit of judgement can be so harmful for us, but it is and now that it had become a part of everyone's behaviour, we must take action. What can you do? Now that you are aware, "stop and pause" whenever you about to judge someone. We have to avoid people who are into too much gossiping, because they will again bring you into the same mud from which you are trying to escape. Changing a habit is difficult, but the more you are aware and the more you "stop and pause" before judging others, the more success you will get in changing this habit.

SIXTEEN

DEPTH OF HEALING

Healing is a continuous process, which continues in phases. The moment we think we are healed from a certain traumatic experience and moves on; it will suddenly come up again making one realize that there is more depth to that part.

Healing, much like life itself, often reveals unexpected depths and challenges as we go deeper. It's a continuous journey that might require us to adapt, grow, and find resilience along the way. It's about perseverance and faith that we will eventually reach that final shore, even if the journey takes longer than expected. Just like swimming through the vast ocean, healing can sometimes feel endless, but every stroke forward is progress. Each wave we encounter can bring us closer to a new understanding or a new way of being. It's about embracing the journey as much as reaching the destination.

Healing is not a straight line going from one straight point and finishing it on the next. It is more akin to an adventurous trek through a series of mountains rather than a straightforward path.

For example, if you want to reach Nilgiris Hills where you want to stay in Ooty, you must pass from other smaller hills as well. Similar is the experience of healing. It is a continuous process and we must not stop in between. You have given so much effort in this journey and stopping in middle is like again starting the journey from the very beginning. So don't stop! Don't give up on yourself!

Keep moving!

There are many depths towards healing. Anything that we are healing can be related to our childhood experiences, adult experience, relationship with a parent or spouse, interpersonal relationships, ancestral healing, shadow work, inner child or can be even related to past life. The more we heal, the more we realize the depth that issue contains.

We were born as pure being, full of love and light, but as we grow our *samskaras*(impressions) also starts developing. Even certain past life *samskaras* can influence our present life. Sometimes these influences can be very strong, affecting us negatively. Until we stop, see it and heal it, these experiences will keep affecting us. But at the end one must know that this is not us, we are not one bad experience or some past conditioning with which we are operating, we are beyond that. We are that pure soul filled with love and light.

We are the fragment of that unconditional source of infinite love and light. We are our own mini-verse (mini universe) consisting of the same quality that universe is made up of. It is a matter of realization and we need to keep reminding ourself of this thing again and again.

I am pure.
I am infinite love.
I am immortal.
I am powerful.
I am divine.
"AHAM BHRAMASMI"

THE HIGHER SELF

SEVENTEEN

BHATKA HUA DEVTA (WHO AM I?)

BHATKA HUA DEVTA
TEMPLE,SHANTIKUNJ,HARIDWAR,INDIA

"Bhataka Hua Devta" is a spiritual concept and temple located at the Shantikunj Ashram in Haridwar, India. The temple is part of the GAYATRI MANDIR and is known for its unique design and spiritual significance.

This temple was made by Yugrishi Pandit Shri Ram Sharma Acharya.The temple features five large mirrors, and visitors often see their reflections in these mirrors, which is believed to help them contemplate their true identity and purpose in life. The idea is to realize that one's soul is a spark of the divine and to seek self-realization.

The concept of Bhataka Hua Devta is deeply rooted in the teachings of Guru Dev, who designed the temple with the vision of helping individuals find their true selves and attain spiritual enlightenment. It is believed that here a devotee or Sadhak can have self- realization by meditating and reflecting on those phrases which are written above each mirror. These phrases are deeply rooted in **Advaita Vedanta** philosophy, which emphasizes the non-dual nature of reality and the unity of individual soul with the Supreme consciousness. Let us know about each of these phrases:

- ### *SOHAM (I AM THAT)*:

Indeed, I am that, whom the almighty has incarnated in human form. Attaining higher spiritual levels is easy for me. I am a Sadhak (devotee) whom Yug Rishi has given an opportunity to perform Sadhna(self-refinement) in this Yug Teerth (Shantikunj). Why should any prescribed task be difficult for me?

- ### *SHIVOHAM (I am akin to Lord Shiva)*:

Shiva means auspicious. Essentially, I am a blessed person; so how can there be any place for evil in my thoughts, feelings or actions? If any inappropriate trait has stuck to me due to bad company or surroundings, it is foreign to my essential nature, why should I have any difficulty in removing it?

- ***SACHIDANANDAOHUM (I am the ultimate being, Consciousness and bliss):***

Why should I be affected by falsehood? Why should I strive for something which will not last forever? I am true bliss; why should I wander searching for material gains? Why not enjoy what is best?

- ***AYAMATAMA BRAHM (This very soul is Brahm: God):***

As the ocean is water, so also a drop is water. Every ray of the sun has the virtue of the sun. Howsoever small the soul may be, it has the capability of uniting with BRAHM; and after union who is small or big? Both tap and tank are capable of giving water so why should I remain small and miserable; why not become all-powerful?

- ***TATVAMASI (You are That):***

Whatever is great in this life, in this world, all of that is you (Supreme soul). Every scene is nothing but light, so why wander searching for greatness? Why become a slave of material things? Why not search for greatness in God and God in all the greatness?"

Isn't these deeply and meaningful phrases? It answers the most sought-after question: Who Am I? These five phrases answer it in the most thought-provoking way possible. It encourages the individual to recognise and realize their true divine nature and to understand that there is no fundamental difference between their soul and the divine consciousness.

When one look into the mirror, and think about these phrases such as SOHAM, it is making the self-realize its ultimate reality. When one reflects on these five phrases daily by looking into the mirror, one can someday reach towards self-realization; meeting their own self, their higher self: ATMADEV.

ATMADEV is not someone else, but you and me. We have lost connection with our own divinity; but the divinity is still inside us just like Parmatma (God) because we are the child of the same Parmatma, hence we all possess divinity within us. In our journey towards self-realization, we find ourself find our divinity: AtmaDev.

When we are able to find that divinity within us, we reach the stage of Self-realisation. We no longer remain separate from Parmatma (God). We become one with Parmatma, where there is no desire, we reach the phase of ultimate bliss, happiness and peacefulness, which then becomes our permanent form.

EIGHTEEN

ATMADEV (A REALIZATION)

Our Divine Self (AtmaDev) is not different than us, this sense of separation creates an obstacle in reaching our own self, but we are not separate from it, we are our Divine Self: our higher version.

AtmaDev always guides us and tries to show us the path towards spirituality. It is us who assume that we are alone in this journey, but we are not alone, our own divinity keeps guiding us only if we are willing to listen to it and receive its guidance and calling. It has only one aim: realization of Self and union with Parmatama (God). But not everyone is able to listen to their own Divine Self, because we are so busy in other worldly things that we lose our ultimate purpose of life. Listening to our own Divine Self is itself a journey and this entire book is trying to cover this journey. Everyone's journey can be different from each other, but at the end we reach here. But to reach here we need to keep refining ourself through Sadhna (Self-refinement) and other spiritual practices. The more we purify and cleanse ourself, the closer we come towards AtmaDev. But there should be no hurry, embrace the entire journey and all the lesson that it teaches us. These lessons shape our personality further and brings us closer to the Divine Self.

The concept of the "higher self" often refers to a part of one's consciousness or spiritual essence that is aligned with a deeper, more authentic sense of being. It's considered to be a source of wisdom, inner guidance, and profound understanding. Connecting with your higher self can mean tapping into your intuition, inner peace, and true purpose.

People describe it as a state of heightened awareness where one can see beyond the surface level of daily life and gain clarity on what truly matters. It's like having an inner compass that guides you towards growth, fulfilment, and alignment with your true values.

Connecting with your higher self can be a deeply rewarding practice. Here are a few ways you can start this journey:

- **Meditation**: Meditation is a powerful tool for quieting the mind and creating space for inner reflection. Find a quiet place, sit comfortably, and focus on your breath. As thoughts arise, acknowledge them without judgment and gently bring your focus back to your breath. Over time, you'll create a deeper connection with your higher self.

- **Journaling**: Writing down your thoughts, feelings, and experiences can help you gain insights into your true self. Try journaling prompts like "What are my deepest desires?" or "What truly brings me joy?" to tap into your higher consciousness.

- **Mindfulness**: Practicing mindfulness in your daily life allows you to be fully present and aware. It helps you recognize patterns, habits, and emotions that may be blocking your connection to your higher self. Simple activities like mindful eating, walking, or even brushing your teeth can be effective.

- **Visualization**: Visualize your higher self as a wise, compassionate figure. Imagine having a conversation with this higher version of yourself, seeking guidance and wisdom. This practice can provide clarity and inspiration.

- **Nature Connection**: Spending time in nature can help you feel grounded and connected to the larger universe. Whether it's a walk in the park, a hike in the mountains, or simply sitting by a tree, nature can be a powerful catalyst for connecting with your higher self.

- **Spiritual Practices**: Engaging in spiritual practices that resonate with you, such as yoga, prayer, or energy healing, can help you align with your higher self. These practices often provide a sense of peace and clarity.

- **Seek Guidance**: Sometimes, it can be helpful to seek guidance from mentors, spiritual teachers, or communities that share your interests. They can provide support, insights, and practices that enhance your connection to your higher self.

Remember, connecting with your higher self is a personal journey that takes time and patience. Be gentle with yourself and enjoy the process.

OUR INNER GUIDE

The higher self is often considered the enlightened, deeply connected aspect of ourself that transcends the ego and day-to-day concerns. It's the part of us that's aligned with our purpose, values, and universal truths. Many people connect with their higher self through practices like meditation, reflection, and mindfulness.It is our inner guide, that intuitive voice or inner wisdom that directs us towards decisions that are aligned with our true self. This might manifest as gut feelings, instincts, or subtle nudges in a certain direction.

CONNECTING WITH ATMADEV

"*Close you eyes and take deep breath in and breath out. Breath in and breath out. Take few long deep breaths in and breath out and slowly bring your attention between your chest centre; Anahata Chakra: Heart Centre. Keep breathing and allow divine white light pouring from top of your head towards your heart centre. Feel it in your heart centre. Feel that unconditional love and a blissful state and request your ATMADEV to show you the path, to be your guide. If you have any question, ask it and wait for its answer. It will come either through some images, thoughts or feelings. Don't be in a hurry. Be patient with yourself. Give gratitude to the divinity residing within you and guiding you at every moment. And your journey towards your Higher Self begins now!*"

NINETEEN

SIGNS OF UNIVERSE

We are never alone in this journey. Universal forces are always there for us, embracing us with their unconditional love, supporting us in our tough times and assuring us whenever we are in doubt. It's our own eyes that cannot see that love; it's our own ears that is unable to listen to that guidance and it's our own illusions that separate us from the vastness of universe.

Universe is always there with us in the form of God, Allah, Parmatama and many more. Universe can be in the form of Lord Krishna, Jesus, Mohammad, Buddha, Guru Nanak, Mahaveer, etc. But his message is always the same: message of unity, peace, love and acceptance for each one of us.

There is a saying that "what you seek, is seeking you" and it's true. Not only we human being is in search of God (Universe), but even universe is always giving us different signs and trying to communicate with us. That's why we are never alone. We always have universal support, only if we are willing to take it.

Universe communicates with us through different synchronicities. It can be finding repeated numbers such as 11:11,10:10,12:12,111, etc. You might see it in a watch, phone, car plate, etc. Have you ever seen such numbers? This is the universe way of communicating with you. Universe has also become technologically advanced to communicate with us. Next time when you see such numbers, stop and pause; give gratitude to universe for assuring you that they have different meanings, it's upon you if you wish to find that out. But one thing is for sure, that each time universe is assuring you that he is there with you.

There can be different synchronicities that you might notice, such as a beautiful fragrance out of nowhere, sudden appearance of a feather at an unusual place, ringing in the ear (not due to ear problem), finding a message just when you needed it, etc. Universe has beautiful way of communicating with us, only if we stop and pause and try to listen to it. Mostly you will see such messages when you are upset or going through a tough phase. Most of us ignore such synchronicities, but those who see it, comes one step closer to God, coming in alignment with the universal energies.

> *"My first sign of universe was seeing 555 early in the morning and after that I received the news of my pregnancy.*
> *Once I was going through a very tough phase and suddenly saw a beautiful white feather in my dream and just when I woke up, I saw the same feather in my home."*

Before that I was not aware of these signs and I had to google it to find out what it means. But this is not simply magic, these are the universal signs, always trying to comfort us, assure us, sending us their love in the most beautiful way they can. But to receive such messages you must believe in these signs. These are not simply coincidences. If it's happening with you, that means you have opened your eyes to the blessings of the universe.

Universe always has beautiful way of communicating with us. We are never alone in this spiritual journey. It might seem tough at times, but we must remember that universe always has our back. So, trust in him and next time when you see such signs, be ready to receive universal blessings.

TWENTY
LIVING A YOGIC LIFE

A life worth living is living a life like a "YOGI".

A Yogi lives his life in contentment and moderation. He has great control over his senses. He balances his spiritual and material life and lives a life filled with joy and inner peace. Majority of us are looking for a peaceful life, but we hardly know the way which can lead us to peaceful living. A Yogi knows the way, he knows how to bring that peace in his life, and he also tries to help others find the same peace.

Do you want to live a Yogic life? Do you want to be peaceful? Do you want to be happy? There is no magic involved in living life of a Yogi, it's discipline which is the most important stepping stone towards yogic living. When one lives a disciplined life, he controls his life and takes the remote control of his life in his own hand. Whereas the one who runs from discipline and consider it simply as restriction gets drowned in the high waves of life and life controls him, he no longer has any control over his health, money, relationship, career, etc.

Sometimes you will find an ordinary person, without any social media followers or popularity living a simple life filled with satisfaction, but his quality of life and happiness is beyond the number of social media followers.

To understand it more precisely, let us take example of Sadhana, he will do his Sadhana every day, without fail and mostly during the same time, because he knows that the energy he is putting into his Sadhana will slowly grow into a beautiful tree giving him the sweetest fruit he had before. So, no matter what happens, except major emergencies, one should do his Sadhana regularly and at the same time. This will help in refining his personality.

A Yogi is always mindful about the food he consumes because the food we eat, plays a major role in nourishing our body, mind and soul. A Satvik food filled with prana (energy) such as fruits and vegetables are preferred. Even the intention and emotion of the person cooking the food can impact the food and those emotions can impact the person eating the food. Therefore, we must avoid cooking during anger, sadness, etc. because our food will contain that energy. That is why a Yogi mostly cook either on his own or the meal is usually cooked by his family member. We all know that we should avoid junk food, the reason is it is a dead food, there is no energy in it. Even food cooked for longer duration contain very less prana (life force/energy), therefore the food that you eat doesn't nourish you, it simply ends your hunger and satisfies your craving, but gives you nothing.

We should eat more fruits and vegetables, freshly cooked food or the food should be eaten within 3-4 hours of cooking, because after that it starts losing its prana (energy). It is often said that when we eat fruits it increases our energy level, whereas if you eat a pizza or a burger you feel lethargic after eating. Another important point to remember is that we should even avoid packaged food, almost most of the food contains preservatives or harmful substances which effect everyone's health.

A Yogi lives a life of routine, with a proper time allocation for everything including waking up, doing his Sadhana, daily chores, eating on appropriate time and sleeping early. He gives time to everything. Sometimes we are so busy in finishing our job or certain deadlines, we forget that even we need to take care of our body, mind and soul. So, take out time for yourself and when you are taking out your times, ask yourself: Have I taken care of my body, mind and soul today? If not, you are at a risk of creating some sickness or stress or frustration, or some mental ailment in long run. So, take out time for yourself.

TWENTY-ONE
SURRENDER TO THE DIVINE

Any discussion about Spirituality, is incomplete with the key to reach to the Supreme God and this key is known as **"Surrender" (Samarpan)**. Unless we learn to surrender, despite doing everything and following every spiritual practice we cannot reach the ultimate goal.

Sometimes we hold ourself too tight and try to control everything in life, but the reality is the more we try to control and want to do everything on our own, the more complex the situation get.

An ordinary living person who knows how to surrender to the divine can reach the divine far easier compared to a person who does all the spiritual practices. This is because he knows how to surrender, he knows that someone is there to take care of us, a greater force (divine energy) is always surrounding us but until we show our ability to surrender, we will not be able to see that divine power who makes way when everything seems dark, who creates a path when we see a dead-end has the power to change an unfavourable situation into a favourable situation.

"Surrender has the power to build bridges out of stone, just like in the epic tale of the Ramayana".

"Surrender to Lord Krishna enabled the five Pandavas to triumph over the hundred Kauravas in battle."

These are not just some stories. This is the power of surrender to the divine whether in the form of Lord Rama or Lord Krishna. We must remember that instead of assuming that we are alone and we have to do everything on our own, believe and have faith in Parmatama (universe) and surrender your worries.

Surrender doesn't mean inaction. It simply means to do the action and surrender the result to the divine. When we take one step towards God, he takes hundred steps to come closer to us. We should never assume that we are alone because his grace is always with us.

"In Bhakti Yoga, this is the most beautiful power a devotee possesses towards God. "Meera's unwavering devotion and surrender to Lord Krishna exemplifies the profound connection between a devotee and the divine." it is said that even the poison turned into nectar, and she remained unharmed which is an example of divine intervention and Meera's unshakeable faith in Krishna. It's a powerful testament to her devotion and the belief that true surrender to the divine can overcome any obstacle."

Surrender is a form of Bhakti (devotion) which we show towards the divine and it makes life easier to live when we know that divine grace is always with us and we are never alone in this journey of life where we will face ups and downs, we will lose people around, we might get betrayed by others, but our constant companion to this journey is the Divine itself.

TWENTY-TWO
SEVA (PATH OF SERVICE)

This pathway towards spiritual journey demands our service. What is this service? It is towards the society. All the knowledge and wisdom, material resources and everything on this planet that we are abundant with is because of this planet, Earth; Mother Earth. If you compare yourself to others, many don't have all the resources and facilities that we are taking for granted. We should not only be thankful for all the blessings, but should also take a pledge to serve others in need. When we serve (perform SEVA), with the intention of serving God and Mother Earth itself, we are becoming a part of the Supreme Consciousness.

Have you ever visited a Guru's Ashram? It's a place where even people in high positions engage in Seva, serving others with humility. Tasks like placing others' shoes, serving food, or cleaning the premises are all performed without hierarchy. In such a setting, no work is considered superior or inferior—everyone is treated equally in the Guru's eyes. This is a profound lesson that we must all internalize: to perform Seva selflessly, without any feelings of inferiority. It mirrors the divine perspective, where we are all seen as equal. Serving and helping others is as significant as offering Seva to God Himself.

Seva, or selfless service, doesn't have to involve grand gestures. It can be as simple as acts of charity like donating food, clothes, or money (if you are financially able), sharing knowledge without charge, or dedicating an hour of your time daily or on weekends to contribute according to your skills.

Seva instils humility in us and helps dissolve our ego, which is one of the biggest barriers on the spiritual path. It shapes us into better human beings by purifying our consciousness and enhancing our personality. The universe operates on a simple principle: ***when you give, you receive***. Now, the choice is ours—are we ready to give, and what are we willing to offer as Seva?"

Heart Talk

The quest for deeper meaning of life and spirituality began with my first book: Divine Message of the Light and it continued and led me to write this book about the journey and lessons that I learned while looking for my own Higher Self. This book is a divine blessing for me. Two years ago, this name intuitively came in my mind, before that I have only read this name in one of Gurudev's pocket-sized books, named,Prateek Upasna evam Devadidev Atmadev ki Sadhna(in hindi) by Pandit Shri Ram Sharma Acharya.

Though I tried writing about it, searching for this name, nothing helped. In fact, there was a time when I gave up the idea of writing this book, because I was not getting any creative flow to write it. I wanted to gift this book to myself on my birthday, but it never happened because I was not even able to start the book. And now that I am writing about it, another birthday is coming up, hopefully this time I would be able to gift this book to myself, giving my heartfelt gratitude to my Higher Self, Atmadev.

This two year is itself a journey of going deep into reaching my Higher Self. Whatever I have written, is the experience I went through, mistakes I have made and the lessons that I have learnt.

My Gurudev, has emphasized on three important pillars of spirituality, which I have tried to follow during this journey, they are:

UPASNA, sitting near God, taking out our time to spend it with our creator, God. This is the first ritual that I want to do as I wake up, otherwise I feel something missing in my entire day. This charges my battery for the entire day to finish all the chores of the day. When you sit near God, Infront of the idol or photo every day, you automatically start absorbing the qualities of God such as kindness, compassion, unconditional love, peace, etc.

SADHANA, refining yourself, to become like God (our ideal), we have to refine ourself, our personality. For example, gold's purification process symbolizes the shedding of impurities—be it doubts, fears, or negative habits. Through introspection, learning, and personal growth, we refine ourselves, becoming purer and more authentic in our values and actions. These transformations remind us that challenges and refining experiences aren't meant to break us but to shape us into the best versions of ourselves.

ARADHANA, an effort to serve God in the form of the society, in which we live, VASUDEV KUTUMBAKAM. Considering God as the entire creation including society, serving him by contributing to the society's needs. God is not merely present inside the temple or Church, he is omnipresent. So why restrict oneself only to certain place to serve him? This entire world, is his heart, let's do our best to serve him according to our potential and capability.

Upasana gives strength to man; Sadhana develops this strength and Aradhana makes it properly useful. One, who follows this process in a prayerful mood, facilitates his path to God realization.

✍? Pt. Shriram Sharma Acharya

When we follow these three important pillars of Spirituality, we reach closer to our own divinity, our Higher Self, Atmadev. Just like the sun gives light to the entire world, our Atmadev is the inner sun who lights up our inner world, he is our companion like Lord Krishna was to Arjuna, he is the divine guide within us, always present to illuminate the path when sought with sincerity, leading us to the divine.

But the most important part of this whole journey towards Atmadev was my Gayatri Sadhana. Chanting Gayatri Mantra either physically or mentally has been part of my daily routine. Gayatri Mantra is the divine blessing that I have received which has constantly supported me in my happiness and sadness, joy and *fear, pain and suffering. I am grateful to have received this divine grace in the form of Gayatri Mantra, which is constantly making me a better person, and has shown the path towards Atmadev.*

The Power Of Gayatri Mantra

GAYATRI MATA

Gayatri Mantra is the supreme mantra of thought purification, leading the devotee towards divine path of positivity, bringing Gyana (wisdom) in their life and dispelling the darkness (ignorance) and leading them to the path of righteousness. One who chants Gayatri Mantra can conquer his fears; there is a divine force which works with the devotee who always protects them without their awareness. The ultimate saar (summary) of Veda is Gayatri mantra, that's why we can see Gayatri Mata holding Vedas in her hand. Every knowledge pond information; all the secrets of universe are contained in Gayatri Universe. For understanding the real meaning of Gayatri Mantra, many lifetimes become less. All the twenty-four letters of Gayatri Mantra contain twenty-four energy centres (powers), which when activated can make the devotee fill with supernatural powers (Riddhi-Siddhi). These powers if you want to understand scientifically, arises within the devotee through twenty-four subtle glands present within each one of us and when these glands become active through the vibrations of Gayatri Mantra, it gives rise to the latent powers of an individual. We human beings possess so many powers, only thing is that we don't have the key to these powers and Gayatri Mantra act as a key, activating our subtle powers. But we must keep in mind that with power comes responsibility, hence we shouldn't take these powers for granted.

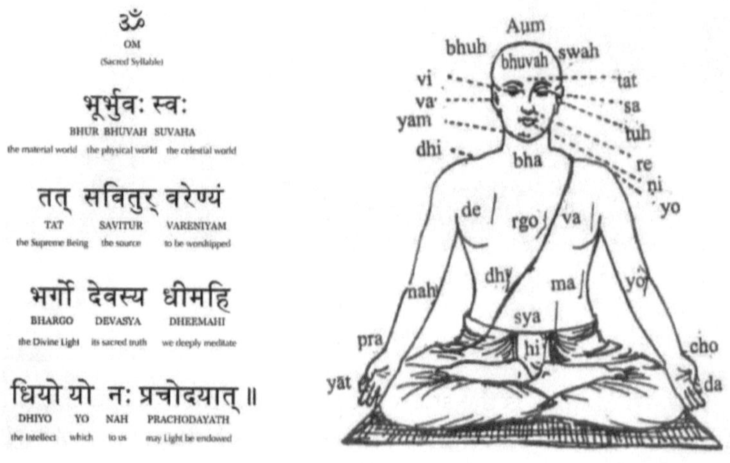

EFFECT OF GAYATRI MANTRA ON OUR SUBTLE GLANDS

Mantra of today's era

Gayatri Mantra is the mantra for today's generation, because this mantra has the power to transform the negative thoughts into positive thoughts. It acts as a filter, allowing positive thoughts to reach Sadhak's(devotee) brain and filtering out the negative one. We live in a world, where everyone's thought is becoming distorted, it's our thoughts (distorted thinking) which is the cause of ninety percent of our suffering. It's one negative thought that give rise to many negative emotions and leading to many actions or behaviours (in negative direction) which are neither good for us nor society.

Therefore, Gaytari Mantra works at the very base of our consciousness: on thought level; when our thoughts are positive, we are able to solve so many issues which are the cause of our sufferings. Our thoughts have the power to either make our life heaven or hell, the choice lies with us. Gayatri Mantra can help us to live in heaven because it is our mind in which we live and when our mind starts working in positive direction, it can create so many blessings for us, whereas when the mind itself becomes our enemy, it can give rise to so many physical and mental ailments, leading us to suffer and manifest as diseases in our life.

Even the society at large is suffering so much because of distorted thinking of our leaders, with selfishness prevailing in each one of us. Gayatri Mantra, through its power to transform thoughts teaches us the principle of **VASUDEV KUTUMBAKAM**: We are all family.

This Mantra is beyond any religion; it is a universal mantra of positivity, peace and harmony. There is so much depth present in this Mantra and as we learn this depth through regular chanting we become a better human being, a better person, a joyful, peaceful and a happy person. This Mantra is like a garland of positive qualities that the divine has created for us and wants us to wear it to reap the benefits of living with happiness, peace, joy and contentment in this world, creating heaven on Earth, which is only possible through our righteous thinking.

An Introduction To My Gurudev

VEDMURTI TAPONISHT PANDIT SHRI RAM SHARMA
ACHARYA-VANDANIYA MATA BHAGWATI DEVI SHARMA

Pandit Acharya Shriram Sharma (1911-1990) was said to be the simplest of men. Throughout his life he owned only two sets of clothes. He began every day with a pad of paper and a ball point pen. And his spiritual practice, throughout his life, was the recitation of a single mantra: **Gayatri Mantra**.

And yet, wherever he went, he sowed seeds that would grow into a mighty movement. Upon the basis of his simplicity was established the integrity of a movement that would renounce the addictions of modern life. With his pen and paper, he wrote discourses on every aspect of human culture and wellbeing that would be translated into 13 languages. And by means of his mantra recitation, he laid the energetic foundation for a new human culture based on the practices and wisdom of ancestral India.

In his own time, he was revered as a visionary, a prophet and a world reforming saint.

(Taken from: **The Real joy of Entertainment by PANDIT SHRIRAM SHARMA ACHARYA**)

GAYATRI MATA

Gayatri is wisdom

Goddess Gayatri is the supreme creative energy of the divine. It endows its devotee with true wisdom. A subtle, uninterrupted current of divine energy starts flowing through the inner being of the devotee, cleansing his intellect, mind and emotions of the perverse, perverted and dark thoughts feelings and desires.

The *Sadhna* of *Gayatri* is worship of supreme knowledge. The effect of sincere and steadfast *Gayatri Sadhna* is swift and miraculous in purifying, harmonizing and steadying the mind and thus establishing unshakable inner peace and a sense of joy-filled calm even in the face of grave trials and tribulations in the outer life of *Sadhak*.

Gayatri Mantra manifested itself through *Brahma* in the beginning of the creation.*Brahma* interpreted it by four mouths in the form of four *Vedas*. This knowledge is for the benefit of all mankind.Persons of all castes, creeds and of both sexes have equal right to adopt *Gayatri Mantra* as means of their *Sadhana*.

Righteous *wisdom* starts emerging as soon as *Jap* of this *Mantra* is taken up as a *Sadhna*.

"*Om Bhurbhuvah Svah Tat Savitur Varenyam Bhargo Devasya Dhimahi Dhiyo Yo Nah Prachodayat.*"

It is a prayer to the Almighty Supreme God, the Creator of entire cosmos, and the essence of our life existence, who removes all our pains and sufferings and grants happiness beseeching. His divine grace to imbibe within us His divinity and brilliance, which may purify us and guide our righteous wisdom on the right path.

Those who tread this path pass joyously through life and ultimately reach the ultimate goal of God realization.

Foundation of New Era through Gayatri Mantra

Gayatri is also known as *Adya Shakti* because *Brahma*,who was born from the Navel lotus of *Vishnu*,was directed to take support of this *Maha Mantra* for creation.*Brahma* worshipped it and performed *Tap* and brought forth all animate and inanimate creation.

This great power will now be known as the power of a *new golden era* because the deadly poisons permeating the atmosphere,environment and minds and hearts of human beings can be neutralized only with the help of collective *Sadhna* of this *Mantra*.The new era is also descending in the form of *Pragya* (enlightened intelligence) movement or *Pragyavtar*.The next era will be known as ***Pragyayug*** (era of enlightenment).It can also be called *Satyug*.

(Taken from: **Super Science of Gayatri by PANDIT SHRIRAM SHARMA ACHARYA**)

About The Author

Kavita Sharma is a Yoga Teacher, Spiritual author, passionate about exploring the journeys of the inner world. Her latest work, "Divine Message of the Light", draws on personal healing experiences and emphasizes divine love. When she's not writing, Kavita enjoys meditation and connecting with nature and doing Yogic practices.Yoga has helped her improve her quality of life and changed her perspective towards life.

Divine Message Of The Light

Author's first book

This book Divine Message of the Light: Journey of the Inner World, explores themes of healing, self-discovery, and divine guidance. The author shares her personal journey of overcoming trauma and finding solace through divine messages, aiming to inspire readers on their own paths to healing and enlightenment. The book emphasizes that we are never alone in our healing journey, as divine support, love, and guidance are always present. It serves as a reminder to seek and embrace the light within ourselves.

Notes

- **Super Science of Gayatri by PANDIT SHRIRAM SHARMA ACHARYA**
- **The Real joy of Entertainment by PANDIT SHRIRAM SHARMA ACHARYA**
- AWGP - All World Gayatri Pariwar
- All World Gayatri Pariwar : ? Upasana, Sadhana & Aradhana
- Impact of intermittent fasting on health and disease processes - PMC
-